I CAN READ ABOUT

BASEBALL

Written by Robyn Supraner   Illustrated by John Milligan

Troll Associates

Way back in 1839, baseball looked very different. Most people played baseball just for fun. There were only a few teams, no uniforms, and . . . no rules!

Today, baseball has a language of its own. It has special words to describe the game and the action. If you don't understand these words, you may be missing half the fun of the game. So here, to help you, are some words that you may know and some that you may not.

BALK: A move by the pitcher that is not allowed. If the pitcher stops just as he is about to throw the ball, or if he drops the ball while his foot is on the pitcher's plate, it is called a balk.

BALLS: A pitch that is too high, too low, too wide, or too close is called a ball.

If the pitcher throws 4 balls, the batter may go to first base. This is called a BASE ON BALLS or a WALK.

1.   **2.**   **3.**   **HOME.**

BASE: The 4 bases are—

first, second, third, and home.

When a player runs all around the bases and comes home,

he or she scores a run.

BATTER: The player who is trying to hit the ball. The batter whose turn is next is ON DECK.

BATTING AVERAGE: The number you get by dividing a player's number of hits by his times at bat. A batting average of .300 is excellent. It means the player got 3 hits for every 10 times at bat.

BEAN BALL: A pitch that is thrown at the batter's head. It's against the rules! The pitcher will always say it was an accident, and sometimes the batter will believe him. A batter who is hit by a ball gets a free base.

BENCH:

A place in the dugout where the players and substitutes sit when they are not playing. A player who hardly ever gets to play is called a BENCH WARMER.

BULLPEN: A place near the playing field where relief pitchers practice and warm up.

BUNT:

A ball that is tapped slowly and gently onto the infield.

CALLED GAME:

A game which is ended because of bad weather.

CHOKE: To hold your hands high up on the bat. This is done when the batter wants to bunt the ball.

CIRCUS CATCH:

A fantastic catch!

CLEANUP BATTER:

The fourth player
in the batting order. The
cleanup batter is usually
a SLUGGER.

COUNT: The number of balls and strikes on a batter. The highest count is 3 balls and 2 strikes. This is called a FULL COUNT.

DOUBLE PLAY:

Getting two men out,
one after the other,
on a single play.

ERROR: A fielding mistake.
Also called a FUMBLE,
a BOBBLE, or a
WILD THROW.

FAIR BALL & FOUL BALL:

A fair ball is one that
stays within the bounds
of the playing field.
A foul ball is one that
goes out of bounds.

FLY BALL: A ball that is hit high into the air.

GROUNDER: A ball that rolls
or bounces along the ground. Also
called a ROLLER, HOPPER, or GRASS CUTTER.

HIT: A batted ball that lets the runner get on base. A one-base hit is a SINGLE. A two-base hit is a DOUBLE. A three-base hit is a TRIPLE. A four-base hit is a HOME RUN.

HIT THE DIRT: Means to SLIDE.
It also means to fall down in a hurry
so you won't get beaned by a bad pitch.

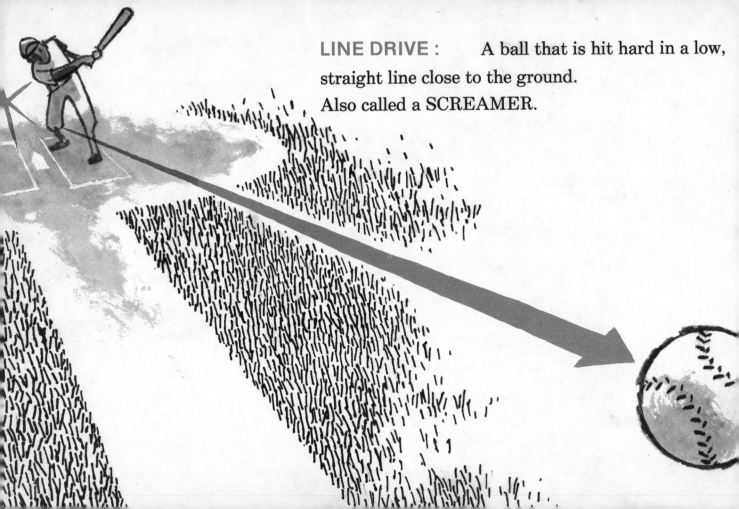

LINE DRIVE : A ball that is hit hard in a low, straight line close to the ground. Also called a SCREAMER.

LITTLE LEAGUE: An organization of baseball teams for young players, with rules and equipment very much like those used by professional teams.

M.V.P. Short for *Most Valuable Player*.
Every year a player is chosen from each major
league to receive the M.V.P. award.

PINCH HITTER: A player who goes to bat for someone else. A substitute batter.

PITCHER: The player who pitches
the ball. Also called the
HURLER, TWIRLER, FLINGER,
CHUCKER, and TOSSER.

POP FLY: A ball that is hit high in the air and is very easy to catch.

RHUBARB: A noisy argument on the baseball field. Sometimes the managers, the coaches, the players, and the umpires all get into a big fight.

ROOKIE:

A new player.
A first-year player.
A player with little
experience.

SENT TO THE SHOWERS:

An expression that means
the pitcher was taken
out of the game
for not doing a good
job.

SEVENTH-INNING STRETCH :

A time—in the seventh inning—when the fans stand up to stretch their arms and legs. There are 9 innings in a regular ball game.

	1	2	3	4	5	6	7	8	9	10	R	H	E
MUDCATS	0	0	0	0	0	0	0	0	0	0	0	0	0
TIGERS	0	1	0	2	0	0	0	1	0		4	6	0

SHUTOUT: When one team does not score at all.

If you win 4 to 0, you feel good.

If you lose 4 to 0, you do not feel very good.

SIGNALS :

These are sign-language
clues that tell a pitcher
what kind of ball to pitch,
or tell a runner when to steal
a base. The coaches and the
catcher give the secret
signals by scratching their
noses, pulling their ears,
or sticking out one or
more fingers.

STEAL: When a player on base runs to the next base with no help from the batter, it is called a steal or a **STOLEN BASE**.

STRIKES:

A good pitch that is not swung at,
or a pitch that is swung at and missed
is called a strike.

Three strikes and you're out.

SWITCH-HITTER:

A batter who can
hit either
left-handed or
right-handed.

TIME-OUT: When the game is stopped for a short time. Time-out may be called when a player is hurt, or when some of the team members want to have a little talk.

UMPIRE: The person who sees that the rules of the game are followed. Usually, there are four umpires in a game. The umpire's decision is final, and arguing with him can get you thrown out of the game.

WORLD SERIES: The end of the baseball season, when the champions of the two major leagues play against each other for the world championship. The team that wins the first 4 out of 7 games is judged to be champion of the world.

Now you know some of
the language and rules. So
the next time the umpire shouts,

"B-A-T-T-E-R UP,"

sit back, and enjoy the game.
Better yet, get in there
and play ball!